MW01026005

For Kimberly,
I hope you will find a
few poems in here that
you like.

Love and Luck
J.

First Edition, first printing 2015 by
White Jacket Press
Copyright © 2015 by Jeremy Reed

Printed and bound by hand in United States of America

Library of Congress Cataloging-in-Publication Data

Reed, Jeremy
    Furniture / Jeremy Reed
    ISBN 978-0-692-43489-5 [pbk]
    I. Title
    II. Poetry

White Jacket Books

Portland, OR
Queens, NY

NUMBER 234

FURNITURE

JEREMY REED

White Jacket Books
Portland, OR • Queens, NY

Acknowledgements

Much gratitude goes out to Ian Abdo and Katy Masuga for their clarity and advice on the preface; and to Margaret Pinard for keeping me on task. As well as to the folks at the IPRC in Portland, OR whose resources and guidance are invaluable to independent publishing in the Pacific Northwest.

Preface

The work in these pages is of and from my twenties, a mercurial decade for sure. Written during a summer and fall in which I was mired in a confusing, ugly, damning little tryst that I let blot out almost everything else from my twenties. I think I wrote to keep from vanishing. I suppose I was also writing to create a landscape for myself. I'd recently shed the one I'd been raised in. I wanted this new territory to be made of a brilliant sheen; or at least the possibility of beauty instead of some middle class pasteboard ruin and its benumbed malaise.

I had developed an appetite for the stark, abrupt revelation. Even though these usually occur in a fit of anger, it seemed to be what was required to free some essential lifeforce from where it gets buried under so much useless chatter, the white noise of pop culture, and the like.

I was willing to endure misery and certain amounts of degradation if I thought an insight was on the horizon. But sensitivity to an inner part of life is as fragile as a soap bubble. It does not survive very long in the presence of anger. I was often in a rush to get down a few words or observations before it faded. Most of the time I used whatever scrap of paper was at hand, stashing these in the pages of multiple notebooks. When I open the journals now these scraps fall out from everywhere.

None of this is a recipe for creating art. Some kind of wisdom, I suppose, would have to be added to it all. My attempt all these years later to add such stuff to the poems themselves only produced what felt disingenuous; an instrument out of tune.

If the poems have any vitality at all, I suspect it's in their contrariness, and their oblique ideas—hallmarks of youth. I have resisted the urge to rewrite them, or polish them too much, for there is useful pain there. Like the characters in them, the poems are graceless, full of contradictions; and are juvenile in their way of trying to explain themselves with a "logic" that is more sentimentality combined with delusion. The poems are a record of anguish. They also seem to represent my instinct that putting a wretched state of affairs into words is a way to mitigate its destructive power. Even now, I don't have a stable conclusion that this actually works. Only that writing down what happens creates a premonition of a return. The scenes, and nights, and conversations I wrote down stir up the same emotions I remember having at the time; but that old degree of torment is muted.

The details sketch out a map; one I can't resist following years later. That territory has grown old, but certain vestiges have remained in place just like any stone ruins; and they remind me how it once was so alien and new.

Whether a record uses words or some other medium, the resulting document exists in mimic of the act of memory itself. So, if we write some words about what is happening, we make an artifact, a headstone, off which our memory can reverberate. Both the memory and this *codicil* become the raw material. Poetry is the echo that passes back and forth between the two.

Woven through the language I find a pre-emptive nostalgia. I must have known the importance it would have in the future. It couldn't have been more than a hazy suspicion at the time. But I remember how its gravity pulled on me as I stumbled through the days, and I believed this meant its influence was valid. And maybe it is. Nostalgia makes a bitter past palatable again. Revisiting old episodes is a way of putting them behind you without having to erase them. Without having to give up what they can teach about not repeating them.

We derive our word from the Greek compound of *nóstos* "homecoming" and *álgos* "pain, ache." A melancholy always exists in the act of revisiting what is no longer. It's a privileged feeling now. The past becomes a hometown (perhaps it's just a cemetery) I carry with me. Yet I meet so many who want and need their own past to vanish from their consciousness, out of some desire to appear sunny and light I suppose; and mostly they succeed to that end. It leaves me wondering how anyone can know them very deeply.

If you are such a person who feels no compulsion to write down your life, I presume you are also someone who can leave the past behind without feeling any sense of loss; likewise you would have no use for nostalgia. Time passes for you without these long periods of emptiness, during which, someone under the influence of their recollections will exist almost entirely in the past while simply going through the motions in the present. You have my envy.

— Jeremy Reed, 2015 Portland, OR

I

[1]   [*scene*]

Deanna calls to see if I want to come over, she explains that
she is trying to set up Nelly and Peter, her neighbors.
They're watching *Titanic* on cable.
When I get there I am given a beer.
We watch the long denouement, survivors
floating in the water.
They have a pillow fight on the loveseat, Nelly and Peter.
Peter is a born again christian and saves gays from the pits
of hell by converting them and healing their curse
through jesus. The lord. He has some hand-book on it,
and everything.

Then Schwarzenegger's doing comedy skits
on Saturday Night Live. "I just love Arnold!" Nelly declares.
"You know, he plays all these tough bad guys, and heroes
in action movies—with all the destruction, but in his life
he's totally conservative. I think that's so sexy!"
She looks over at Deanna sitting next to me, but really
she's sneaking a look at Peter right next to her on the loveseat.
… he stares at the tv like it's fascinating… like it's an alien.
Well anyway, says her posture.

Then Tom Petty plays a new song.
The camera shows the rest of the band.
Deanna says, "I like *that* guy. With all the hair…"
and looks over at Nelly. That side of my face goes hot
like I'm next to a fireplace. But I might just be full of myself.
So I also stare at the tv.
Then we all agree, at the end of the song,
that Tom Petty is cool.

They have another pillow fight; then Peter gets up,
straightens his hair, and his V-neck sweater,
bids adieu, and leaves abruptly.

No one speaks. For several minutes
the tv is the only thing moving.
Thank god we have something to look at.
It's very quiet between the three of us.

Nelly gives some signal with her eyes and gets up,
mouthing a few words to Deanna like a mime
before going out the door herself.
Deanna laughs when she uses the spare key she gave her
to lock the door on us from out in the hallway.

The stairwell creeks as she goes up to her apartment.
Deanna calls her on the phone
after putting the sofa cushions back in place.
They discuss the possibilities for her and Peter.
She keeps her voice low and goes to sit on her bed.
She motions me over and pats her hand on the bedspread,
putting a finger to her lips—he lives right across the hall.
They want to know what I think, if Peter likes her.
Yeah. It seems so.
"He says, yeah, he thinks so." She listens, turning aside.
Then, "Okay I will," and hangs up.
Her bangs veil her face a little.
She looks at me through them. "Could you hear what she said?"
"No, what was it?"
"Nothing. She was just being weird." She yawns
and takes off her shoes.
"She made a comment that she left, and you're still here."
"It is kind of late; should I go; you want to sleep?"
"I don't know." She inspects her thumbnail.
I ask how Peter came to do what he does.
She says, "I don't know, he's from a really conservative family."
"Nelly likes that, huh."
"Yeah. I don't get it, but…"

I ask her what she did before she moved here,
what her life was like. She shrugs, "I don't know. Usual stuff."
I feel like an interrogator. I'm about to go.
She says wispy and maybe hurt: "I'm just not
the kind of person who talks about themselves. Unless someone asks."
I ask; highschool days, what bands she listened to,
what crowd she ran with, prom, …anything…
Her answers are short and vague, she doesn't care about them.
She seems annoyed, pinches a crease down her pantleg,
keeps her eyes down. Sighs. Curt. Irritated: "There's some wine
in the door of the fridge if you need it!"

"Wine?" I look over at the kitchen. Nothing was clear to me.
I get up and move toward it slowly. I stand in the cold humming light.
"Do you want some, too?"
"No thanks."
Glasses?
"None are clean."

I bring it over and sit down again.
It's a big bottle, and awkward on the small bed.
I tip it up, swig from it: trashy, but nothing else. Good god,
it's white wine. Cold, flat, sticking to my throat,
making me stale, too. She lays down,
puts another pillow beside hers.
She points out: "I'm going to fall asleep. You
should do something to wake me up."
"Want me to rub your back?"
"Wow! Nobody's ever *offered* to rub my back before."

That's how it begins

[2]

My footsteps touching the sidewalk; and the ticking of water drops
on the pavement, falling one at a time
from all the trees
along the otherwise quiet street. The going of time.
These two sounds, together.
I don't want anything else with me
in the changed night... what I mean is:
night, the thing that it is, has turned into something different
than what it has been for all the years of its incessant recurring—
all in the past now.

There is over my brow a soft, living light
that lingers at the borders of recollection:
The night's beginning...
in her apartment, after Nelly leaves, I feel myself shaking inside,
a mind full of disbelief and the sparkle of uncertainty,
and from the other hemisphere a blinding
undeniable certainty pouring warmth and paralysis into my face.
I am verged on laughing out loud at being included in something.

... ...

and feel, particle by particle
my flesh and everything that is
my body dissolve in the warm surge
of flattery coursing through it,
going along the otherwise quiet street—
which is here around me, belonging to my footsteps,
but I am still there watching Nelly go out the door
and lock the bolt from the hallway,
and sensing the gleam of a candle flame
swivelling in a pretty glass jar on top of the tv set.

... ...

as if I couldn't be a real thing at all;
no kind of thing I ever knew.
As if I couldn't really be walking just now
beside this otherwise quiet street.
This night something other than a copy
of a thousand before it.

So. The strange memory
still wet from its birth,
must be a flattened fantasy, brittle.
While it refuses to be flattened. Dangerously unbrittle.
          … unlike the others in my head…
Wild color surging all across the ridges
of that dry mushroom inside my skull
that soaks it up unsorted.

The rain gathered
in the trees goes

plick

plick

plick

                    … the trees
animating a little   brush back and forth in the breeze,
they blur in the orange glow of the lamp-post.
The sky all rained out,
its desultory clouds remain in place for tomorrow.
Slow moving night bugs in the wet soil under a leafy hedge
stop their work and watch me going by, my shoes anyway,
and are touched by a thought:
if they were to get crushed by them,
all of what they've encountered will remain tomorrow
what it is tonight.
Their destruction won't hinder or harm the world.

Against a dark background the drops continue to fall
silver from a leaf or a power line,
or from the eaves of apartment buildings, and so on
one at a time, etching a slow rhythm
of your going
toward home through the neighborhood
you will now have a nostalgia about;
which cannot be shared, only exposed.

While in your mind, in similar dark,
in a room,
one of your bookcases is falling over
a bit happily.

[3]   Twist

The aftermath.
Clothes and everything scattered everywhere.
… "I feel like I lost my keys," she says. "Have I?"
"No, I don't think so."
It's all silly.
"Okay. We have to sit up now, and talk about this…
here can I wear your shirt?" She puts it on, and lays
a cool pillow across her naked lap, folding
her legs together under it.

"Remember," she begins, "at the bar a few nights ago, after class,
when you said you'd probably date like three people?"
"If it became like this with someone I don't think
I would want to date other people."
"What do you mean?"
?   "…do you, want to know what I think of you?"
"Yes."
"I like you. I genuinely like you, how you are
in class when you speak up, what you say. And I think you're pretty."
The blue in her eyes changes. She backs away. "I think
that's the nicest thing anyone's ever said to me."
"Well, I'm sorry, people should've said it more…"
She is pretty, but maybe doesn't know it—or more tragically,
doesn't feel it. But what girl…
Do I know any girls who actually feel it?
'…some wine in the fridge
if I *need* it…'? Jesus. What a thing to say.

"Am I a girl you would want to date?"
"Yes."
"Do I remind you of anyone?"
"I don't think so."
"Someone from the past I mean."
"Oh…" I shake my head. "No."
"Good." She is relieved; but it isn't enough.   —I see it, like
a lake that continues to drain, terribly: predictions dawning.
Her eyes change back, she keeps them away.
"I don't want anyone else to know about this.
I just don't want them to know. Anything about it."

I hear the word okay come out of my mouth.
Then I say, "Do I remind you of someone?"
"Yes."
"Oh," I say, like I get it. I wait. She doesn't elaborate.
Her face has changed, too; it's mechanical now.
She begins something else, something other, distress revealing
the line of her jaw, eyes hard, looking me over. The appraisal.
Something familiar after all: She asks, don't I have
a mirror. "I mean…," she begins to assemble the words.
She is far away now and I feel it
coming over me, yellow red and sick. It makes me
                    weightless
          in fact.
She is saying, her hand out like a pointer,
"…you're just… you're anorexic," her hand
almost touches me, as proof, but withdraws in time.
"No. This is— " my voice tries to get out from under a rock,
finding-stumbling a few words here and there: "— I've always…"
She laughs, dry. "No! You *are* though. I mean,
I don't know *why* it is. Maybe you're
just too broke, or you for*get* to eat, … but, I mean
there's no way you could be in a relationship right now."
Swiftly, in the time it takes for a night
to pass in the snap of fingers, I become an old role—

See,
I had moved away from my hometown, to a new city.
But the role followed me, apparently. It's a skin.
It's opaque on me. With someone new
I can deflect for a little while,
long enough to feel like it's gone, but this
is a ruse. It's the same here, too.

I'm slow to react. All I desired
was to get angry, but I didn't find it anywhere,
the rest of my thoughts disappear. Full of disdain as I watch…
myself going along with the surge of her voice,
as a shadow of it in fact—hoping
my refusal to take part in this weird argument
will facilitate a release of the pressure, her rage,

but she gets a storm going, then it's too late to push it back.
I'd let the moment pass without jumping into
the fray, she sees. Her rage doubles
the way you might beat a stray dog for its obeisance
after it finished the initial batch of charity, and then developed
some milky-eyed expectation.

Unsatisfied, she keeps going.
She says to my body, its ugliness had accused her,
and exposed her somehow,
as ugliness up close often does, she says to it,
"I'm a nice girl, Jeremy! I don't do *this*," sneering,
the desperate, low-class tinge of it, "I don't *sleep* with my friends!"

Rather quickly—like a lightswitch—I don't care, which
makes her seethe.
Words are a newspaper I am throwing away,
and the thoughts with it.

I couldn't find all my clothes. She handed some to me.
They were dead rats to her.

[4] The Dive

You go head forward, down,
through a curtain of smoke and haze,
until the light narrows out behind you. Deep
into the artificial light of the bar; flies
rustle as you approach, ruined old heads turn, then
all of you together settle into place. They with their Luckies,
you with your Pall Malls.
These barflies. You believe in them.
They who have nothing to offer,
and no aspirations,
have no reason to steal from you.
They have ruined themselves to the point of sainthood.
When the dark door creaks open, a soul leaves. But we stay.
We're on a ship that went down years ago.
No one is in love here, they
never heard of it, and no story about it is credible.
Or even interesting.

Its absence doesn't feel like absence.

The mechanics are simple.
There are the taps, there is the tv.
Sometimes a clock to look at now and then.
There is the bar, the chairs, the carpet.
Smoke rising and rising.

14

[5]

I sit in the back rows of classes
supposing my way to A grades.
Each day I sit here I fill in one of those mint green pixels
of the attendance ledger.
If I keep going like so, I'll graduate.

It's all some miserable kind of excrement.
We are to know that Shakespeare
is all about language, and masks…the two being versions of one thing
that we have no word for yet.
You put one on, and are someone else,
nobody thinks any different. The world
addresses you as the name you declare from behind the mask.
But take it off and you are stuck
with yourself and suddenly culpable.
How profound.

Yes…
but how doth one better the lesson? How apply it?
Is it not a tool, oh yea, but it travels so,
and we are but the trees light and wind
blow through. My mind doth only trouble;
and thoughts, do they only meddle?
Better I meant that they were of steel,
but this too only leads same mind to think
that I meant of thievery…

It's all some miserable excrement.

[6]

Back at the bar we are all there,
when I go to flick off my cigarette ash, it falls
as I realize the ashtray has been moved, and as I
notice Deanna moving it back before it hits the table,
and the ash floating in like the flotsam from an exploded star;
rushingly I know in my mind that it is just like that
sometimes. And if you don't believe it's a sign of something cool
then what will you ever have?

It's a Thursday and none of us have class tomorrow.
Belinda is happy-hour-drunk, "Braid-girl so wants Chest-hair;
it's so obvious, too, she tries to come to class
late so he'll be there already and she can sit by him,"
laughter is making its rounds, we all know it's true.
"But Chest-hair only wants Deanna!"
Deanna says, "Oh does he?" She's like a sick cat, won't look up
at anyone. "Why isn't he here then?" her eyes distant
and tragic again, blue and steel and like a metal ocean.
Even Belinda quiets down with the rest of us,
all in reverence to a dying.

Every shirt Spencer owns is cut to display his chest.
Also, according to Deanna, "he has the same hair
as my favorite artist."
He also has the small spectacles, the James Dean stance,
the cigarette stuck in the corner of his pout.
He's a cardboard cutout of Jack Kerouac.
You can imagine the crap he writes
for all us Plebes to listen to in class.

She'd started buying books by writers he'd mentioned
he read once,
and I bought books I'd heard her talk about.
We spent our money that way, for awhile, the two of us.
Me, not to carry the books around
like merit badges of intelligence to show
how similar we were, but to know her. Yes. A little.

It's impossible to have anything to say.
I've been good and obedient about not telling anyone, per her request.
I believe my fidelity in this
will be rewarded. But like a battleship
docked in a pond: Jealousy.
I know it's distasteful. I put it in a grave
I keep for such things. It doesn't help.

Then she's in a bad mood,
filled with disappointment that Spencer hasn't been
very responsive to her flirting techniques.
He's called her up a few times, but never accompanies her out.

And yet she spent so much time reading all
those books she must not have enjoyed.

[7]

When you called me anorexic
and added alcoholic because the first thing
wasn't satisfying like you thought it would be,
I was waiting for you to finish me off
with
masochistic freak.
That's the risk, I suppose.

But I think maybe you said those things
at a time when you felt threatened
by something,
either by me, or by something else,
or someone else, by the past? Or by not getting
what you wanted the way you wanted it, and knowing
the unenchantment of having to ask.

Another night... saying that I was the consolation prize;
that you had big plans for someone else;
"You are not the one I'd
been hoping this whole week
would be in my bed this weekend!"
A dark cold liquid.
I'm angry that I'm surprised, an itching starts deep under my skin,
I don't go to class for a few days, food disgusts me—it seems
I might prove you right after all.

Days later you call,
and I'm so ugly in myself I'm hopeful,
and light, my muscles flutter
as I pick up the phone; I knew it would be you;
so I go over, and it's all the same
as before, and I'm one of the things
in your apartment, the same as your chairs,
and that dumb ottoman
you think is so retro-chic.

You love a bit of clutter, giving the annoyed sigh,
kicking one thing or another out of the way.

20

It's like practice.
I cringe to hear how much television
is in all of it; if you were to follow your *mis en scene* with some
rubbing of your fingertips over the bridge of your nose,
another sigh,
and start a sentence with "Look…"
I would pulverize into dust.

[8]

There is the dramatic afternoon sky with clouds
shuffling into place for the downpour,
dusk to follow, and the quickening of nightfall,
the wheeling clouds as they shift like ships—
a dulled silver covers
the streets and sidewalks, glossy and muted,
even those oily tough-fiber leaves that suspend beads of water
in their valleyed spine, making them seem artificial, are twisting with
life
as the rain beats on them. Twisting to catch the silver of the waning
dusk light
like a flash.

Here in the bar it is good too.
I can't help feeling like, falling in love with being
in an Edward Hopper painting. I keep this cliché
to myself while it rivers through me.

Mounted on the fake wood panelled wall there is a frame
with a chord coming out of it that goes down
to a socket. Shimmering, the lit-up image of a river
made by snow melting off the mountains
in the background. The river doesn't worry
whether it might some day be unable to support
the life that returns every spring, and no thought
occurs in those fish brains about the water
becoming too toxic to be safe for them.
There are fiber-optic sparkles that make the river
appear to ripple, and then there is the clock face too,
its 12 3 6 9 and blunt black wands over the top of it.
It's all so cheap and so obviously plastic
it isn't intended to fool, but only make a joke of itself.
What a stupid thing to envy.

[9]

I chide myself, my shallow intolerance.
We all want
the acceptance of unconditional love
while we practice
no acceptance of any but those
who would be our near copy.

[10]

Then the tv shows are over.
Suffering through the faux emotions
of Ally McBeal. She turns off the tv set.
The kitchen emits a soft amber light
from behind the partition—the light over the stove top
alone in there.
All the light is well placed, organized here.
The hardwood floors dark and wet with shine.

She says, "You know, if you don't tell those things about yourself
because you think no one is listening, someone is. I am."
It's easy to believe. It's like starting anew.
This is a fatal flaw.
Knowing so doesn't help. My mouth is opening
and I am telling a little more.
To be unknown is a terrible thing that blights you.

She asks if I've ever read *A Moveable Feast*.
"Everybody who wants to be a writer
should read it." She reads the part about F. Scott
being a butterfly, and his talent the dust there on the wings
being marred then revealed to him,
but his love of flight gone from him.
She has a good out loud reading voice.
The words sound good, almost like they are things
with smooth edges and bevelled planes.

"But, you have the biggest void of all," she says. "It just
seems so. You're the observer. You fill your void
with people."
"Is that why you think I'm an alcoholic, too?"
She laughed, the first one of the night.
"You mean when I was calling you one the other night?"
"And the other things."
"Why do you let me treat you so bad?"
"I didn't see it coming. It was unexpected."
"Even after the first time?!"
"Maybe I learn something, or think I will, when people
are like that."

She picks at the bristles of a hairbrush. "Sometimes,
I say things I don't believe just to get at you."
"You could ask."
"It's not the same."
"How come?"
She doesn't say, or want to say.

"It makes me sad, talking about all this stuff," her voice
smooth and dry again, a smoker's rasp laying lazily
just beneath the tones that, when boysterous
become harsh like metal boxes slamming together.
Self-hate tries to push its way up my throat, but I
pack it down, an old skill.

I could have left, but this was all like the desert at night,
and I wanted to know what was out there.

[11]

I'm eating Chinese food near the window in a big booth
that is empty and confuses me with having to know it
so much that I can't taste the kung pow, and
anyway have to also feel the cold of the too panoramic glass window
breathing on me but there is no wind outside,
only laughing couples on their way to a party.

Revealing yourself to the wrong people
is a self defeat, they will exaggerate
how much they don't care about you.
It's the lack of identity
she wanted from me
the lack of the personal.
They need you to be a function only,
as they work out their own issues—long abandoned
and now pushing through their membrane
like a war they have come to lust for, but fear
the mess, the blemishes incurred.
Empty: they want.
The whitewashed.
The rinsed out.
The blank.

Sweet fragrance on my hands from the bathroom soap

like someone sitting next to me.

The waitress, young, tired, annoyed
and with one arm in a sling walks by,
her steps light as a crane's, to leave the check
and the cookie and the mint.

So much time ahead,
like a block of concrete: my face.

[12]

Blue dim reflections of our arms, legs folding
unfolding like waves of water
warm and sense-less
numbing but warm
waves that knew you and thrilled.
Waves without pressure
or sharp edges.

That could not drown,
or if so, would make
it peaceful.

[13]

We seek the depths of our nature
through its corruption.
It's the only conduit to an
unnatural world, a deeper self.

To be too far outside the epicenter
either of an earthquake media event, or
a fashion debut media event,
is a torturous regret. (for example)

And yet,
this large movement toward
spiritualism, nature,
body-mind-soul.
Deeper selves should be everywhere all around me.
Instead it is gimmick, plastic joy, thin angers dissolving and cresting
over and over, ever and ever.

Feel the night's dark sparkling net
feel the night sky rise
by a single cord like a circus tent.
No funeral can happen here, all are
sleeping—the next day building in them as they dream—
except lovers—a year builds in their sleep.

[14]

She didn't like undressing in front of someone
unless they had more clothes off of their body
than she did. I was down to my jeans, I pulled
the top button apart tentatively,
she remained still; amused; staring; her head cocked.
I stopped.
She shrugged, jerked her bangs aside,
pleased, grinning half way, lightly.

Reaching for my shirt now trying not to feel
looked at. Or let it show I felt looked at.
She makes a disgusted, victorious,
sound in her teeth.
Still, doing me a favor. Ostensibly.

"You're an easy target."
"Does that mean I need to be destroyed?"
"Maybe."

[15] ... Low...

It stays light outside so late now.
Someone painting thin, light grey
water color over blackness.
It will lose, surely,
but succeed momentarily.
You've vowed to someone
that you are going to lay off the booze,
but go into the bar to order drinks
for your customers up the corridor in the humid diner you work in;
the safeness of home is there while you wait for your order.
The briny odor of the mildew rises from the rubber mats
under the bartender's feet, a scent that is like the fullness
of a memory you can't escape, and don't want to.
Coming back with their drinks
naked and alone—surely it's easy to see
as I dissolve into the complacent chatter of safe topics
and pointless utilified communication of flaccid notions
to make patrons feel they are appreciated.
While in the dim closeness
of the bar, the silent keno screen and the haze and the music,
its warm hands: something cares
and has no fear of its expression.

Just above the low hills the width of a hair ribbon, the horizon
is a near colorless glow,
the rest of the sky arches unfathomable through every
shade of blue, and of light to dark, punctured in a half dozen
places by a star that you wish was a something
that was looking at us from there, and knowing more than we do.

On the other corner, inside the bus, the bus's glow
with its stained hard chemical light
you can see the forms of all the people you wish
you were going somewhere with.
You watch it lurch to a stop and creak open the folding door
the sound echoes across the intersection
and some people get out and disappear up the street,

into the dark following the sound of delight made
by their own voices it seems,
their night already set to a memorable one for them.

[16]

"What does it matter what we do now!?"
She's breathing fast, like some terrific thing is dying
and needs to be rescued, and no one is moving.
"Who's keeping track?" — snapping the cigarette
on the ashtray-rim. No one says anything.

"…and anyway, we meet the same people. Later.
So we have a chance to do it right the next time.
We have this set circle of people we keep on meeting.
…there are some people
I don't see anymore,
don't write to or anything.
I never will.
I wouldn't change any of it—even though
some things are… they're just like," she puts her palm
on her chest over her heart, then brings her other hand
in a fist up to it to touch the back of her hand.
"I learned from it.
So why would I regret?"

What we do when the cold pink pain of ecstacy and defeat
go coursing through it, even though we know, we have
learned repetitively that the hand—or the fist—or anything
it can hold or bind, are all entirely incapable
of protecting what beats beneath, what beats to stay alive
and the bruises it creates.
"…but, I don't like being near the edge either. I've talked
to these two about it." Belinda and Lewis. "You've probably
noticed on your own," she says to me, also looks at Charles,
but he shakes his head. "Anyway, I can't talk to Jeremy
about it," she laughs and Belinda and Lewis smile, get cigarettes going.

"It's because I know I could take that extra step and be dead.
I could take absolute control and do it, just to have it.
I guess I'm afraid of heights, not because of the height
but the control it offers. If you ask, most people
aren't afraid of the height, it's the other issue."

In the car, me and her.
Spencer hadn't shown up.
"You pick. Are we going to my house or yours." She started
the car, and the night sky sparkled like champagne
through the windshield.
Her place is nicer.
Into the pause she says: "One time is okay, right?"
"Yeah," clearing my throat, then, "Your place is nicer."
She laughs uneasily. "I like my place! Are you making fun of me?"
"No. I'm really not."
"Good. I don't like it when people are sarcastic." She drives out
of the parking garage. "Did you bring something?"
"I have something with me."
"Boy! You sure think quite a lot of yourself!"
"But I don't! Not any at all. I just feel what I am
is alright; you made me feel alright just now when you asked
who's place we should go to."
She makes a curt sound I can't describe.

The books are in a stack on the little table.
Spencer's reading list. His personal syllabus for her.

[17]

Why is it always crowded when you get high?
Everything becomes sharp and foresty
and important.
Lewis plugs in a laptop, nods when it comes on;
but there's nothing in any of the files. A focus of some sort
mildly sharpens his features.
The screen glows bright as an idiot. It stares back at him,
its got the glow of an imbecile.
Then he sets it away from him on the desk.
It's too heavy, he never carries it with him to class or anywhere.
Doesn't that make it a desktop? I say, barely
getting the words out I'm laughing so hard,
the joke occuring in my mind faster than my mouth,
falling off the arm of the couch
onto the cushions helplessly convulsing.
I'm saying repeatedly, This whole fucking thing!
This whole fucking thing! My god! This whole
fucking thing!

He pays no attention to me.
When the screen goes off he touches a key
to make it come back on.
Well, there's nothing in the files, he says. I guess. I don't know.

We're going back to the bar. Everyone
high enough, he asks before we endeavor to depart.
Anybody want something else, it's early,
we can always get something else.

You end up just going home.
In the morning you know
your choice was correct,
but all you feel is bad,
and empty.
You feel like the end of something.

[18]

You call me to come over. You say, and I do,
like you knew I would; you know how simple
I am. And you tell me to bring that poem I've been working on.
You'd like to read it.
It's a different world. I can feel spring and summer
mixing in the sky.
While a mellow weak-lit dusk hovers
motionless and waning in the spaces
between the orange strips of clouds.

I am carrying my poem
and my feeling of my poem, this one about my family,
that I've tug-of-warred with, and been spun by,
and surprised by,
and I think I am saying something in it now, the final draft.

Enthusiastically you are pouring wine in two glasses
and moving around your apartment which has had the furniture
moved since I was here last, and there are more lamps.
Maybe it has been a long time.
And so we drink the wine and there are candles going
back and forth liquidly in their delicate glass cylinders.
It smells nice like you have just perfumed some of your clothes.
Then the window is dark blue, with the night sky hushing down
onto the streets of this neighborhood that must be something
to really talk about in the future.
Then the door knocks, a slight tremor in the hand tapping against it.
It's unlocked, you say. Come in. And Spencer is here.
And I see everything as it is supposed to appear to him.
The two empty wine glasses on the little table
in front of the loveseat we sit on. I watch him notice them
and the candles all around the room,
and he maintains a smile that reveals nothing
to me, to you neither, I suppose.
As cold as I feel in my stomach, I am appalled to see myself
helping create the suggestion you want: that this is a soireé,
that in no way were you just sitting around
in your apartment awaiting his visit.
I can't get up right away, like I know I'm supposed to,

not because I want to make it difficult for him,
or even for you, I'm afraid of embarrassing
myself—I can't feel my legs, except just to know they are there
laying out from my hips on the couch.
The wine turns to lead in my muscles.
Now I look at the bottle and see it is empty,
and in the nervous unpaintable quiet, cigarettes letting
threads of smoke out... the only sound,
you snap the bottle up and pour out two drops into my glass
perhaps as a gambit meant for him to see
that we finished the whole bottle,
and just how casual this all really is for you, to see
the actual measure of his significance.

[19]

When you get home there is a sign hung on a strip of tape
across the doorway of the elevator. It reads:
    the Elavator
    is Out
    of Order
and you just want to kill yourself
for all it says
and doesn't say.
It would be so easy. Giving in.
You lift one weightless foot and step toward
the open elevator shaft
and begin the leaning
the letting go of it, all of it...   the ...lovely drift.

You find your feet going down
to the end of the mediocre hall
and start up the stairs
to your wretched depository of a room.
Because you don't follow through on anything really.

[20]

Then it doesn't matter if you write to remain
in the world after you're gone.
It's too crowded already anyway. Remaining
is not a presentable machine.
It would matter more if you rush it
and make it balloon into something not yours at all,
and join the under 27s; but you haven't achieved anything
and 27 is coming up fast.

It matters if you sit in the good light
of bars chain smoking, your dumb face
between the pages of books already written,
and to show, even if only in your mind, that you feel a moment
is passing
each time it lays down next to you, next to your elbow,
on your knee et cetera et cetera... the good light I'm talking about.
The little strip of it coming through a window
or the crooked door that doesn't close right.

You have to visibly ruin yourself so bad
that when they read the things you've been
writing and hiding they might not seek to slay you,
they might try to see what
you are in spite of yourself.
But people are so falsely strong, and it takes too long, and when
they find their desire to know, they're in a hurry to consume you,
like a piece of a... or a delicacy... or something.

When people talk about their life,
they tell you all the decisions they made,
and thus derive how things became so wonderful,
even the weather turns great, apparently.
It's simple, they say, you have to find something to do
that makes the world a better place,
and then you become a better place.

[21]

"When I would drive home after class...
you know, one night I passed by your building and thought,
'I should call him. I haven't heard from him in awhile.'"
And so she's calling. I don't have any response.

"So... You didn't enroll this term?"
"No."
"How come?"
I'm deciding what to say, and how much. Whether it matters.
"It isn't because of me is it?"
I could have pushed over the walls of my ugly
little room easier than what was needed to resist
saying anything here. What might assuage the worry
in her voice pushed against the roof of my mouth
to force it open. But I win out over it this time.
She says, "I feel bad, you know. So, so bad. There's so much
we never talked about."

"I do want to explain, you know," she says into the silence.
"Oh."
"Maybe we could meet. Next week..."
"Alright. I won't have any conclusions until I hear what
you want to say."
"Thank you. Thank you." her voice like a truck downshifting hard.

48

[22]

You say you made time to tell me your explanation—
        but all you talked about was every little detail of your affair
        with the older man who said he'd leave his wife,
        and who you locked out of his own car to stall him
        as you fled—

And having me trail you around the mall the whole time
as you looked at a plethora of things you didn't even want.
"It's really sad," you were saying, "I guess. But I'm not
going to feel anything for him. It's stupid.
The *it's sad* is all his. He lives it now. It belongs to him."

Afterward, on the miserable and humid bus you press yourself
in against me, imploring me to talk again; "Say something!"
I say, low, almost not even speaking, "I don't
think I believe in love really."
You wrap my arm in both of yours, excited, "I know!
Me neither!" You jump on everything I say,
claiming it as having been your own
for ages. Your victory is me
similar to you, no matter how ugly it makes me.
I was getting sick with the rocking of the bus, the steam
of everyone's smell roiling around heavy and slow,
becoming a taste in my mouth,
and you wouldn't move. Shrieking instead: "What?! What is it?!
Tell—me—what's—wrong!" The whole bus looking, even
the sedate ruined bums raise their heads. Of course
you like me this way; and that there's an audience.
Scrambled and like a white-out inside, I needed off that moving cell,
away from you. My eyes, betrayingly, started to swell.
I start getting up, even though
you are like some fortress in the aisle seat,
you stay sitting there. You shriek again—What is it!
What are you doing! Where are you going! You
have to wait for the bus to stop Jeremy!

The driver looking in his special mirror
at us banging on the back door—god! he wanted
us off that bus.

II

[1] Ghost Story

Trapped.
A body of memory,
unshedable.

All ghost stories have the same apparatus.
Someone is removed, trapped
and kept separate from
the rest,
seemingly forever—this is the torment;
having nothing to do—for life isn't available
to them and no death either.

Always asking for help,
they don't know how to tell you what to do,
they only know how they got where they are.
They keep repeating the tale, the only thing they know.
Their ability for language has been removed.
They rot, and look like us, and never age.
Stasis, misery in every gesture: each one leading
to a cliff, an endless cataract, where the beginning
emerges all over again.

They can only disturb, beguile, terrify the living,
their big desire is to disturb their own cycle, their trappings.
The only person who can free them
is the one who put them there.
Both are trapped. Sometimes.
Though plenty like it this way,
it gives them power
they have no other way of getting.

[2]

Belinda. Drinks too strong.
A tab is engaged.
You want to recline, or be supported, lean
on the edge of something that holds
you up, like a drink used to, or a cigarette.
She's a Taurus, she's saying, "...the thing about Taurus is
they're very understanding. It can suck
because people are always unloading on them.
You can push and push, but when it's too far
it's really bad. For everyone."

I want to ask if she's seen Deanna lately, but
if I ask what she knows, I'll reveal what I'm not supposed to.
I'm still keeping quiet.
I'm afraid the dam will break if I start
to talk.
She's saying something about Lewis.
I ask if he is coming down for a drink, too.
"Have you *talked* to him lately?"
She asks the question in a tone like she is wondering
if I had any awareness of reality. She explains.
"See, he was talking to me about his ex-girlfriend,
like getting back together with her, like
toe-tall-lee testing the waters! To see if I would escalate
things between us, like if there was more there with us,"
she's building up to a laugh. "I told him right out, 'Hey, great,
it's perfect. I'm in love with somebody else, too.' And I mean,
he started crying!" A burst of coughed laughter through her
gaping smile. A satisfaction at being able to see him like that,
and being able to spread it around to others who know him.
The laugh, nor the smile; I couldn't match.
We get more Cape Cods.
It makes me want to hang out with Lewis just now,
or some other fallible human beings;
not with people who are brimming over with
all the goddamn answers to everything.

[3]

As much as me a horse is alive
in the wet street.
Surely this is a dream,
but the horse eyes me, going past, lifts its head,
the damp strands of the mane shake and settle heavy
down its neck. Nodding, it snorts,
a kind of word, ...surely this is a dream,
but the horse has eyed me,
it moves down the street.
Does anyone hear its feet striking
the asphalt and all the echoes
off the sides of apartment buildings.
You don't get looked at in dreams
don't hear echoes.
There it is,
but how so.

This cannot exist,
it is what I carry inside.

The sky is cloudless and starless and infinite.
The trees are still, and not even the disaffected youth
who sleep in the park are here to ask for a cigarette,
or sixty-one cents.

I stand on the precious brick walkway
glossy through the shadows of the park
wishing the insipidly wonderful chiffon colored light
would do something to my shoes.

[4] Greyhound

It takes so little, I guess,
just say some stupid pat thing about affection,
and peace, use a phrase like "the world…"
and put some cliché about the heart in there,
and a shrug and a grin and a gimmick,
and get self-deprecating and awkward and
she'll feign sleep and let go of herself, her muscles,
her legs open with the swaying of the bus
and she doesn't move when the skirt is slid
above her thighs, a lace hem of her panties
glows in the shadow between them.

Across the aisle they're developing
a connection. I appear asleep, more or less. I suppose.
But he doesn't seem to care too much either way.
She moves, finally, waking, yawning, stretching her arms,
I see her large dark eyes, she looks at her bundled skirt
like it's a cat that stowed away on the bus and is sitting
in her lap now, in love with it.
She doesn't roll the hem back down, buckling
with laughter instead, and looking into his face —

>I saw him eyeing her at the station while she fumbled
>with a caché of batteries for her walkman. Then he sat
>next to her when everyone boarded the bus,
>and they started right away with the usual chatter.

>It takes so little. Really. Say something already a copy,
>something about heart, peace, the world. And beauty,
>don't forget beauty. He spoke of the world's beauty,
>big and everywhere, as if it were molecules themselves.
>Of course *American Beauty* has come out.
>People are already cribbing what that guy says
>about that goddamn plastic bag.
>It's fresh enough that it still works here and there.
>Another month it'll be totally worn out.
>But that's why people go to movies.

—— she's nodding and laughing,
and her dark eyes sparkle in that dingy
overhead light, and she's dropping the barette
she took out of her hair and reaching between
his legs to find it again... one of their arms
reaches up and clicks off the light.
And now it's a big rolling coffin.
And the lace edge of her panties glows
in the wave of moonlight coming in
the windows of that side of the bus.

The coffin has made it safely.
We're pulling into a town, the sordid edges of it pock by
on both sides of the bus in the heavy dawn.
All the different license plates. And the condensation
filming the inside of the windows.
The guy wishes we would get back on the road;
she would feign sleep like she does so hot,
and his hands could explore, deeper this time.

The sun noses over the hills and the windows
on one side of the bus become opaque.
I'm sad about the trip being almost over, too.
I could go another two or three hundred miles
of not being in one place.

[5] Time

The fear that it's true that people don't change.
It will always be a repeat of all this.

You disappear years at a time
and demolish yourself
and reconstruct
but it's the same again.

And the fear that it's not true
that people don't change,
and that it's you anyway. Something fundamental
that gives others no option
to be otherwise.

The fear that any method you devise
won't lead to a useful notion.
Fear that she's right, I need to be destroyed.
That it would correct an equation so it could be solved.

You make your exile long this time.

You sneak back to town,
two new generations, with their own hammy names and nuances,
have come onto the scene, the stage, whatever.
Spates and spates of new tv shows
just for them—the emerging market share.

And then it's the same again.
Fear, not because the world
is full of people like her, but something
fundamental in you
gives people no option to be otherwise.
You see they aren't this way
with others.

What is it?
How do I kill it?

[6]   Echo

…and so I did.
I met the same circle of people again
later,

different names faces masks voices.

All ghosts
come back
from time
gone by.

.

62

[7]

Looking out a window at the sunset begin pale,
and then flame with color without a movement
of any kind, just color emerging along
the ceiling of clouds now showing
its furrows in the cloud field.

The borders framing your vision disappear.

The sunset exists only to sow
this color
that vanishes now, but hesitates
just so,
flaming up a little first, just to get you
once more.
The color emerging there as if it had always been there
but a trick kept you from seeing it,
and the moment you notice it has turned red from orange,
it is already receding back to where it was concealed.
You barely have time to point it out
to someone, and anyway they wouldn't
see it the same and wouldn't want
to see it with you there ruining it
with your dark sense of how it only
appears so it can show you how it can only
vanish.

There's such a terror in seeing it,
it wasn't made for you, since it only fades away;
but a photo of it is comforting.
When the older man told her he was going
to leave his wife, he stepped out of
the photo she'd made of him
and into her kitchen where his hard-soled
dress shoes made their sonorous clump clomp
clump at the bottom of his shadow and his
disgusting ears at the top, his coffee-teeth when he
smiled painfully at her.

[8]   How To Know Your Age

I write at the top of my sheet of notebook paper.
It's a new notebook from the grocery store.
Then I begin the list of ways
to know such a thing—I mean,
to know it as a time that is hard to define with borders,
but is different from the one in the future,
in which you will look back and see a fixed age
like a number that will never occur again;
and you will know all sorts of other things besides—
and knowing all of these will make it impossible
to be treated like furniture.

And, perhaps even as I write this list, a worm
of dread crawls through what I see—
that when I "know things," as I've put it, when I'm wise,
I'll miss this younger self who was so willing
to be a part of all sorts of demeaning sickness, and to live
with a bloom of ice physically in the stomach; because the same
happens with love after all… people tell me.
The wonder and fear, come over me at once
like a strange, bright, but leaden shimmer
as I conceive of the idea of coming to know it, like a delicacy,
once I finally perfect a complete list.

No genuine sadness exists in metamorphosis—as Kafka
attests—only the false kind,
welling over you, even as you know it cannot be authentic.
Only memory and nostalgia are here,
and excitement and dread too, like breezes that change the weather.
You are fuller, heavier, are less believed
if you try to claim naïveté, your old hiding apparel
now a shiny costume:
— the list I've made stares back childish, and un-childlike,
    employing clichés, not once being authentic.
    But you know it can be done, such a list can be made,
    just not by you, your limited intelligence.

[9]

Dark night tonite, no moon,
wind tries to make off with the curtains,
throwing them back into the room
in anger.
They are irresistable,
it returns with an altered strategy, twisting them
up a certain way, but with the same results;
while its lusty cousin in Florida
will take whatever it wants.

Lights out,
let the cigarette pinpoint
where the two axis meet
simmering:

A space must be there
where light and dark
touch edges and is neither one.

In the "nowhere" you engage in metaphor;

wander in a thought-fog;

invent language that doesn't translate to others.

[10] Misery—fulcrum—Lovely

The lovely times take our innocence, too.
We don't feel it going, changing, so we are to
believe we still retain it. What fools.

The lovely thing is the more dangerous
for all its flowers and cake
frosting, like a dream.
… we don't feel it going, and turn tricked
and a bit airy like a spring color out of season,
it can't be touched besides, so what use is it.

… and not feeling a change must mean it's a beneficial one.

Misery challenges you to come up with
what you don't already have, and makes it impossible
to come up with anything new
until you revisit the past
after it has been the past so long
it is weary of you like you are of it.

You may not know you need a wealth of this
to return to, to see what an imp
and moron you were in details
that could only belong to you like an odor.

Even a lovely time will change your innocence,
making it impossible to have the same beauty over again,
which was only ever possible because
of that untouched naïveté with which you
submitted yourself to the scene whether it would
turn out to be lovely
or misery.

And this belief just the manifestation, after all,
of a dream you had in childhood when your mind
held fantasies of dramatic events
leading to such deep sustenance and a shimmering glory; the mind
though even in youth, already aware that you were not

going to be a sparkle
on the eyes, and the unnameable instinct that
you were going to have to develop some inner
labyrinth to entice anyone, expands.

Knowledge itself a dark garnet.

[11]

Then it's years
all over
again,
seasons seem clogged in drains.

I happen to see him in that burrito-bar attached to Mary's Club.
Some while after I didn't see any of them any more
I had wondered how long he would stay in the group,
and the gust of absence that goes through me—
like it all just happened—takes everything I thought
the passage of time had built. It was all dust
evidently.

He's having trouble ordering. He's got
that young-old face pressed together under
a layer of wax that's trying
to preserve his youth: it's face it's card,
but the wax is caving in
with his flesh.
And it seems his arms and hands
operate by shaking and clumsiness.
He's a junky now.
He wants a burrito, or more truthfully,
he is aware that he can't remember
how many days went by since he
last had food going in his mouth.
The girl at the front counter is patient,
assures him his beleaguered indecisiveness
is fine, "It's cool. It's fine, you want it the way you like."
He speaks slowly, the words like boulders he has to move
with his palsied tongue.
Then he asks again about the limes,
whether they're fresh.
Yes.
I mean *cut* today.
Yes. Every day we cut new ones.
You don't save the left over ones?

No, we give the left over ones to the bar
for them to use.
You're sure.
I'm sure.
Okay. You can see I love limes.
Sure. It's okay. You want it the way you like it.

He tries to push the electricity of his thoughts
into shape by a force of will
but it's weak, and very little of it is sensical
as it comes out his throat, his dried out
chuckling voice, trying to smooth everything over,
and she, this minimum wage nurse
has to guess and gesture the meaning
with her hands, telling him
in an asking-like pose, what it is he wants
in his burrito
as he stands transfixed by
the bright colors of the bottled jarritos in a bin of ice.

He has an automatic family
with so many people now,
everywhere he might go and whoever he might encounter.
At least he did something against his despair.

You can see I want the needle,
I want to be him, or just
with him in the same raw day
that never gets defined by time;
it rolls through you as you roll along the curves
of its endless saxophone notes.
It might be the only day that ever existed.

I already know I'm too much an outsider,
and to try to join in with that experience
is a false gesture
crumbling to pieces the shell of my fantasy.
So, watching—consolation
in watching.

The white hot light in the doorway goes
cool and blue when two officers come in,
in no hurry, and move their blade shaped sunglasses
up to the top of their steaming heads;
their radios ruffling the air with the volume turned way down
so the official jargon being spoken from them has the small voice
of a broken wind-up toy far away.
They are not here for lunch we can see, and they move
toward him, and he turns to give his dark wrinkled eyes
to them without fear.
Without any fear taking place anywhere in him.

[12]

Then the art show I don't know how I got to,
but was, I confess, in search of some kind of scene, art or
otherwise; at the height of my despair, or depth of it,
however you classify the end of things.

It's horrid and miserable, it matches me deliriously,
and so awkward am I at this thing I do wish
I was already junky, this time the wish is like a stiff
icy wave pushing against something in me, a glass
wall or some such thing, preventing the wave from doing what
it's supposed to do—continue on inexorably; or whatever.
And it's all so—delightfully now—horrid, art school.
The students, the neato dandies, flashy and posing,
and then I realize how preposterous it all is, everyone here,
except myself, is a mother or father of one of these dirigible-headed
urchins with paint and clay lodged under their fingernails, they'd
rather have a finger cut off than clean the "materials of proof"
out of their nails.

Good grief, the whole thing is a giant
refrigerator with proud mothers and fathers standing
among the might-as-well-be-magneted pieces everywhere
you look. What purpose, then, is there to sending one's kids
to art school. I'm so atrocious I want to buy each of them
whiskey, and help them to the gutter to clear their own eyes
about themselves.

I've turned. I've become. It's awfulness doubles as I view
this development as progress rather than defect,
my misery and defiling gaze on these works,
some of it probably has merit, and deals with authentic
inner selves that are lathe-ing and warping and spinning
off to gentle destructions, and adaptations, but my soiling eyes,
and my shaden-fraud
only prove she was utterly clear and correct in debasing me.

The work assaults me, asks me to give from myself
to these pieces, to a something "arrived at"
but not thought out,
not seen, except for that initial spark of an idea.

So miserable, these rags of painted board and flannel…
This one a jagged mess: the lines
scribbled during an earthquake
apparently, or on a city bus,
all the lines going somewhere, in flight
as it were; but none of them with the same
destination.
I read the card and it says
he was trying to convey what it is like
to have an epileptic seizure, and that the
final painting, as also true for all the previous versions
and preliminary sketches, and studies,
is a failure.
It can't be conveyed by any means outside
the actual experience of it
itself,
and that is why in this final version, the reason
he was comfortable submitting it is that
he painted in the word: failure;
in unstylized, basic, block letters.
I lean toward it from the waist, push my glasses closer up against
my eyelashes, blinking hard, slow,
and see it at last, the letters black on one edge,
white on the other, and painted over by a thinned out gruel color:
that is the palette for the rest of it.

It's the only thing I love. This painting.
I want all his peers
to notice how superior and honest, decimatingly
honest this work is. For a moment I wish I had epilepsy so I could
warmly nod
and feel something in— then I stop before I let my meretricious
patronizing go too far.

Here I am envying his epilepsy, I know,
it's reprehensible, disgusting even; as I've already said.
I try further self-recrimination, but it's all just
rhetorical devices.

(fuckall)
I envy it,
knowing what it is that drops him into his vulnerability.
I envy it and him and what he did.

But
won't he develop over time an acrid disdain
for the fatuity? It's like melted butter, the easy kindnesses
everywhere, even those not being utilized for gain...
A dark mood even against kindness?
I stand
a long time in front of it
trying to draw attention,
refusing to step aside when other gawkers
approach, some giving me a condemning look
as I sway, and breathe vodka fumes everywhere,
nearly tipping over against the paintings hung beside it.
Do I have any decency at all—not stepping aside,
like only I exist here, comments are ventriloquized
in my direction through tightly shut lips: probably by
the father of the little monster who painted all
those apples nestled in a brass bowl next to it,
ostentatiously the largest canvas in the building,
which I suppose is meant to be the statement.
!*Art School*!

Finally,
I angle out of that palace of entitlement
onto the hard wet smelling pavement, lights leaking glazed
uncontrolled across the surface; ah, here is my fresh air.
I push the button for the crossing signal.
It begins to rain.

Waiting is the last thing I remember.

[13]

Surely
some answers
are here.

It's like
looking at the stars to explain the stars.

[14]

We encounter those who encourage passion
only if it takes place in a small cell,
or the confines of a brick room,
its expression does not belong
in the world.
Passion is good if rendered powerless.
Passion the invisible core of a fire;
enthusiasm, the light from the flames.
A lightless fire is acceptable for so many.

[15]

Seeing Belinda's face fall, as she sits alone
in the pleasant conundrum of a scene she's a fixture in,
but not really a part of.

This is how I know I am not an alcoholic,
I see things;
and this is how I know
it doesn't matter if I'm garbage.

It also proves not to matter
to know such things.
Victory is right away a kind of space
with nothing in it.

It's never been a dream to be a part of it
I tell myself and leave.

[1]   [*outline*]

[a poem on the experience itself being what you miss after it ends,
even if it was terrible; it was so formative, you miss, and cling
to, the sensation of developing from nothing into something.]
[It should be visceral. There should be no mention of plants,
flowers, breezes, lakes or oceans, not even rivers.
No sky. Of any kind, sun or moon either, just the things that
happened, described as their visual selves. No metaphor or similie.
It can't be full of wispy language, and nothing esoteric, or exoteric
either. It can't have any of that 'either one thing or its opposite' shit.
[More of a demonstration like putting stone objects into place with
each other. And nothing sentimental, and not a lament either,
not just some list of complaints or it will be grating like a noise
a person is making in the quiet of the library, worse because it's
unnecessary, also irritating, incessant.
It has to be a clear presentation of the actualities, what happened,
like the ancient Greek architects nervously, and bravely, supervising
the construction of what they'd drawn—the stones settling into
place with a canvas bag of sand under them and the laborer up on
the scaffold cutting the bag in particular places to let the sand
run out so the heavy piece of marble settles just so in its niche—
making a mistake could result in death. Maybe some of the stones
have a design. Nothing ornate. Simple markings. And all in
the bright light of the day.]
[And something about how we reward innocence with opportunism.]
[But not a monument, or any of that shit that sets out to "honor the
experience." It's more of an assembled group, a presentation that is
alive like theater and when it's over nothing remains except the
recollection of those who watched it happen.
And it can't be in the first person or none of the above will be valid.]

[2]

only once are you truthful like this

How to proceed